Every Word Was Once Drunk

Poems By

Ian Bodkin

9/27

Barbara,

May we always
be Pretty and
near Rivers.

—

ELJ Publications, LLC ~ New York

ELJ Editions Series
2nd Edition

ISBN: 1-942004-03-5
ISBN 13: 978-1-942004-03-5

for Honey who always reminded me that I was a rascal, for my Mom who rebuilt a mountain that I could call home, for my sister who taught Drunk to walk around that mountain before he spoke, and for Wendy who took in a boy that knew how to kill spiders & made him a poet willing to raise a child

CONTENTS

ACKNOWLEDGMENTS

Portions of the poems in this collection have been published in the following journals: *491 Magazine*, *Handsome Journal*, *Borderline*, and *Misjudge Your Limits*.

INTRODUCTION

For many of us born after the mid seventies God was always too far away, the need for heroes had much less to do with Sunday and more to do with Saturday. As children we were introduced to Superman, the last survivor of his alien race set to become Earth's greatest champion, and Bruce Wayne, a young man who took the violent loss of his parents to fuel his path for revenge and the redemption of his city. Both of them wore masks, Superman's became that of a mild mannered reporter, and Batman donned the mask of a bat to become more symbol than man. We were introduced to their abilities, we learned about the events of their childhood and the reasons why they had to fight to preserve the better parts of our humanity. Just as these *superheroes* could not engage in the world without a mask, for many poets, it has been necessary to create a persona far more engaging than the pronoun "I" or the common nouns of mother and father.

According to the Oxford English Dictionary persona is defined as "the aspect of someone's character that is presented to or perceived by others," and for the literary definition it states "a role or character adopted by an author." In terms of poetry, *The New Princeton Encyclopedia of Poetry and Poetics* defines persona as a distinction going back to Plato and Aristotle between "poems or parts of poems in which a poet speaks in her own voice and those in which characters that she has created are speaking." The article continues in pointing out that persona can be "used to refer to a speaker who, though obviously not the poet, is a spokesman for the poet" and since the inception of modern psychology namely the work of Carl Jung persona is described as "the self a person assumes to play a social role" (*NPEPP*). In Latin and Greek the word literally means "mask," mainly because Greek actor originally all wore masks for their given part. Within each definition the idea of an intermediary is presented, the mask is a voice between the under lying self and the outer world; what I allow the world to perceive the self or "I" to be. Whatever the audience or the reader comes to understand about the persona is an instrument of the poet.

In looking at the most basic idea of the "mask" or characters the poet may pursue, the dichotomy between Superman and Batman provides for a unique entry point into the concept of poetic persona. On the one hand there is Superman, refugee from a distant sun, his true name is Kal-el, but after being raised by human parents, the Kents, he creates the character of Clark Kent to protect his true superhuman identity. Playing Bill in the Kill Bill movies, David Carradine describes Superman's conundrum as follows:

"Now, a staple of the superhero mythology is, there's the superhero and there's the alter ego. Batman is actually Bruce Wayne, Spider-Man is actually Peter Parker. When that character wakes up in the morning, he's Peter Parker. He has to put on a costume to become Spider-Man. And it is in that characteristic Superman stands alone. Superman didn't become Superman. Superman was born Superman. When Superman wakes up in the morning, he's Superman. His alter ego is Clark Kent. His outfit with the big red "S", that's the blanket he was wrapped in as a baby when the Kents found him. Those are his clothes. What Kent wears - the glasses, the business suit - that's the costume. That's the costume Superman wears to blend in with us. Clark Kent is how Superman views us. And what are the characteristics of Clark Kent. He's weak... he's unsure of himself... he's a coward. Clark Kent is Superman's critique on the whole human race."

Now in the movie, Carradine's character is making the argument to Uma Thurman's character, Beatrix Kiddo, that the majority of humanity is weak, and just as Superman cannot stop being Superman, Kiddo, a born killer, cannot stop being a killer. He is right about the inability to escape the nature of the self. However, the alter ego of Clark Kent is not Superman's critique of humanity. True, Clark Kent may be the way Superman sees human beings, nevertheless, Kent has a human mother and father, Kent grew up and went to school, Kent is a reporter for the Daily Planet, he has an apartment, surely a few bills here and there, a bank account or two, and it is through Kent that Superman loves Lois Lane. Superman puts on the suit and the glasses, and yes it is his "costume," but more than a critique, it is how Superman, Kal-el, the last son of Krypton, interacts with humanity. Once Superman has stopped a nuclear missile from hitting the city, or an asteroid from destroying the planet, he does not hang around, he changes into Clark Kent to get a beer with Jimmy Olson, and it is through the mask of the mild mannered human being that he is able to truly interact with the world.

On the opposite end of the spectrum is Bruce Wayne, born into aristocracy, head of a major corporation, Wayne Enterprises, and for all intents and purposes he is a member of the elite, the upper echelon of American society. However, due to the loss of his parents as a young man at the hands of a petty thief, Bruce Wayne takes an all-together different path than that of the typical 1 %. Unlike Superman and countless other superheroes, Bruce Wayne does not possess super human strength or speed, he cannot shoot lasers from his eyes, a bat did not bite him in some experimental mishap, and the same holds true for gamma rays or nuclear radiation. Bruce Wayne is human, thus so is Batman. If his butler, Alfred, brings him a whiskey at the end of the night's patrol and the Joker creates a riot in Blackgate Penitentiary, then Batman will have to leap back into the Batmobile and likely ruining his buzz. The desire, the need to put on the mask, is a choice Bruce Wayne, the mere human, makes consciously.

The choice is two fold; first, Bruce Wayne decides to fight crime. Randall M. Jensen, associate professor of philosophy at Northwestern College, points out in his essay, "Batman's

Promise," that the decision to fight crime goes well beyond Bruce Wayne's revenge over his parents death, he explains, "whereas [Wayne's] philanthropic parents fought crime by improving Gotham's infrastructure, Batman takes the fight to the streets. This suggests that Bruce wants not only to atone for their deaths, but also to give meaning to their lives by ensuring their legacy doesn't die with them." As a child Wayne watched his parents give money to the poor, and through Wayne Industries they had tried to improve the lives of those less fortunate by building clinics, affordable transportation, shelters, etc. But for Bruce the problems of the city—the poverty, the hopelessness—are the broken windows in the warehouse district. Wayne's own loss of hope comes from watching his parents gunned down by a random thief. If chaos can steal from our lives, then why can't an agent of chaos return if not our safety, but our sanity?

The second part of the choice is where, for me, Bruce Wayne becomes more of a poet than just some vigilante. He decides upon the mask, he chooses to become a symbol as well as a means for justice. In Frank Miller's graphic novel *Batman: Year One*, the story begins with a twenty-five year old Bruce Wayne who has recently returned after many years abroad honing his combat and detective skills. After failing to defend a young girl from a pimp one night as merely himself and a bit of makeup to disguise his face, he has made it home beaten and bleeding. While sitting in his mansion he begins to talk to a bust of his father, when a bat comes crashing through the window: "I have seen it before… somewhere… it frightened me as a boy… frightened me as a boy… yes. Father. I shall become a bat." In these briefs clips of thought, Miller is telling us so much about the nature of Batman and what the symbol means to Bruce Wayne. The bat frightened him as a boy and now will be the figure to fulfill his desires. The need for Bruce Wayne to say this to the bust, and in many ways ghost, of his father shows the importance of this decision. As Carradine says, Bruce Wayne does wakeup as Bruce Wayne, while the identity he chooses is that of the bat. He may be known to the world as Bruce Wayne, but he reaches out to that world and identifies with the mask of his own creation, the Batman.

Outside the panels in the humdrum of our daily lives, we are not altogether different. On any given day, we will wake up. We will have breakfast or forego it, make coffee or tea. We will dress, we will prepare ourselves with rituals or routines we have cultivated over the years to step outside of the house and into the world. Through this action we define our selves and our own reality. We choose to smile, we choose to frown, we choose to remain stoic. We present to the world who it is we believe the self to be. The world reacts to the variable of our demeanor, as our demeanor is affected by the structure of the world around us; a reality is formed.

The OED defines reality as "the state or quality of having existence or substance," which is pretty abstract. If we go to the ever popular Wikipedia they elaborate, explaining that, "in a wider definition, reality includes everything that is and has been, whether or not it is observable or comprehensible." So whether or not we understand it or even notice it, reality exists? I would also mention in terms of defining reality that I am banned from editing Wikipedia articles after listening to Stephen Colbert on his February 1, 2007 broadcast and trying to change the definition of reality to "a commodity to be bought and sold" on the website, which in hindsight I believe still corresponds with all the other definitions here. Nevertheless, we are not in dire straights, only experiencing or understanding the absurdity that is existence.

For my part, I come from a long line of mountaineers and hill people stretching through Appalachia from the Virginias and part of the Carolinas. I come from a swath of folk who like to speak aloud and when they speak the closer the mason jar to their lips. To drink or imbibe is a communal act done around the campfire or out on the porch on a summer night in the mountains while fireflies light the air and crickets bounce their symphony from one tree to the next. Just as the figure of the bat is a way for Bruce Wayne to match the face of his father, and

Clark Kent a costume to honor the human parents that raised Kal El or Superman, I wanted these poems to make reference and honor my Appalachian heritage, if only in language and symbol.

In the creation of my persona, Drunk, I began simply with the word *Word*. Not the one of biblical proportions, but the unassuming noun. At first, these poems were just small limericks or notes jotted down on some scratch paper to the side of my laptop. They were mere musings and experiments where this expression, designation, place holder, could get up and actually react. As with most things, I was influenced by Whitman, in particular his poem, "To the Sayers of Words," where he writes,

> Air, soil, water, fire—these are words;
> I myself am a word with them—my qualities inter-
> > penetrate with theirs—my name is nothing to
> > them

I wanted Word to be a figure, a symbol, something relatable but altogether separate. It began without gender or understanding of the world around it, our world, my world. The noun was just waking up and we were introducing ourselves.

As the poems formed around these thoughts, the very footprint on the page took shape as well. None of them contained titles because they always felt like a series of field notes. I was just a documentarian out in the wilds of my language writing nothing more than studies. So each poem began to form around an opening unrhymed couplet, then as if in notation came the inset lines beneath. But every study is a song and I needed some way to fade out before the next one faded in and thus the phrase in a handful of syllables, like a signature of the executor to the right of every movement. Of course, as the poems collected themselves, even this frame began to mutate and alter itself when needed.

Then for years I'd add ten pages to cut out twenty. My Word was a poem, my Word was an animal, but I needed my Word in all his adventures to be every possibility of humanity, if not a bit maligned. I could see his palm-prints like the caves of Chauvet on the page. But the word *Word* was too iconic, too biblical, too mercurial. I could see the path my mask had taken, but I couldn't make out the visage.

At the time, my wife was drawing a series of abstract sketches with bars and grids and forms askew to the page they were drawn. One of them had this large opening near the center like a hole at the bottom of a nest. While I kept trying to figure out how Word could be human because again there was no radiation, no animal bites or secret origins from some unknown planet, I pinned it to the wall next to my desk. And there where my eyes could rest, I thought of humanity like fire, but that came from the gods, which left it six days after Word. I wanted my mask to be immediately human, like Clark Kent, I needed my persona to stumble, but like Batman I needed it to still be a symbol. I wanted him fully aware of his faculties, even if they were out of his control. So I wrote there in the negative space, Word I think you're Drunk.

—Ian Bodkin, 2014

"Every word was once a poem"—Ralph Waldo Emerson

"Every word was once an animal—Emerson"—Ben Marcus

Preface

Honey in her rocking chair, a sigh
to take the mind, another starlit
couple unravels at the inevitable
of her magazine. While we wait
on my father to come take us
to the store, I'm learning to shuffle
Hawaiian playing cards; fire & rock
to a slow stutter in clumsy hands.

A breeze or question against her
front door—just swung open—
"Company's coming," she smiles,
licks her finger & turns the page,
as I think about the whole
declaration of it all, my Drunk

                              in root.

#1

Drunk enjoys honky-tonks, back
room holes, service in mason jars;

       passages of highway sun,
       eyelids of starlight, for days
       nothing is said so when
       he asks for ochre & a cave wall,
       the room drops dead. Drunk
       explains absolutes, they

                          dance till morning.

*

Drunk is a pair of hands that do not
hold with feet that cannot touch;

       in a pattern of ocean from interlocking
       landmass to the water at the door,
       an incoherent grumble repeated,
       the storm that took an entire humid
       mountain by river & valley settled,
       God is best miles away in a motif
       of light; the sound is confusing while
       a single root remains below the cliff;
       with teeth clenched, Drunk is ready
       to open, respond
                      & fall from.

*

Drunk does not meet the needs or memories
found on the local & all too familiar;

        a spring path downward en route
        to a shed, & the legs that burn
        with something close to fear are maybe
        five—the memory says three,
        but the limit is a perception—while a man
        recognized with the symbol "father"
        & later dubbed Illogix sits many little
        legged paces up the mountain
        sipping on a cup too large & too strong
        for mid morning; the young Drunk
        is a cold burn in the back of the throat
        with each foot the choke, "hacksaw, hacksaw…"
        till he stands before the drawer of saws;
        Drunk walks back up with ten jagged edges
        & not one hacksaw, Illogix drags the child
        back down; Drunk never forgets
        the difference of saw blades & twenty
        odd years later his jaw

                            still pops.

*

Drunk carves masks for composure
with utter diminutives of hellfire;

        the phone reaches a pitch & substance
        rings out as an echo, one more imitation,
        what is said can be highlighted & gone,
        tap of delete, static of agency
        listening for the buzz words with notes
        to decipher the context: plane, over,
        bomb, patriot, down, down. Drunk is
        often paranoid in the air & mischief
                            in opinion.

*

Drunk is an emergence of false
or so the balcony audience whispers;

> on a couch, the greatest figure
> is Bruce Wayne, furor as he plucks
> at his polymer bat ears, smeared
> black liner, painting a target on
> his chest-plate because a cowl does
> not protect the mind, lots of flapping
> about & always the low croak
> when he says, "*from the shadows*,"
> but the billionaire-I'm-a-playboy
> -with-a-bottle-in-my-hand-focused
> -on-buying lilt with a chilly crack
> that defines an anger of release
> toward a killer & state today, "*I saw*
> *Joe last night*," To an orphan
> of murder Drunk nods, taking
> notes: mask is an imitation. Nothing
> less than

the possible.

*

Drunk stood on the stage waiting
for the curtain & silence to come down;

>   the ancient player with a cloak
>   to hide his backside & all the scars;
>   a mask, the intent of expression;
>   the crane conjures flight. We are
>   imitators married to imitators—
>   old men sip their wine & attempt
>   to drown the performer or destroy
>   the mysterious bend in a calf,
>   neck, or tongue from those distant
>   salons, assuming the answer of the
>   thousand faces passing below
>   —all the while Drunk spits & sneers,
>   Plato, Plato!

*

Drunk picks the same twelve steps
over ten years on an un-strung guitar;

> *It's just a little out of sight*
> *as I'm driving this old Ford*
> *I'm already out of mind*
> *need a tank of gas or more.*
>   The bridge.

                                   The trouble is in the bridge.

#2

Drunk appeared the submissive servant
printed above the swinging door;

      a lick left with sign on the rim,
      symbol cracks within the glass
      each sip a conservative thought
      Drunk adheres to a collage of
      rapt labels with long-

                            -distance tumblers.

*

Drunk is hyphenated with specks
& glitter to hide the high holy;

> the response is a hand to dead
> men's tongues, heroes glorified
> for death, & between the sheets
> Drunk is alive

singing scripture.

*

Drunk hasn't spoken to Illogix
for weeks, he thumbs the dial;

       Illogix likes to talk Illogix,
       how the world is organized
       against him, he pauses with
       questions of Mother Orchid,
       Drunk is a chorus of mm-hmms
       who mumbles I love you

                             states Good-bye.

*

Drunk culls him a disorder hired
to find the agents of substance;

> squelch devours a passionate
> hush in the rhythm, squeak,
> the war cry of feedback obscures
> what notes the mayor & the town
> draw in the fresh concrete & streets
> end in stereotypical dead-ends;
> the song is a pitch, bridge, or love
> away from Drunk's ears
> > & its loquacious
> > > stockade.

*

Drunk imitates action, covers what is,
some whole, like a living organism;

> thirst runs with dogs beyond the break;
> thirst is within every shadow, lovers
> have faces beyond recall; for hours bodies
> dripped with sweat, rooms in shambles,
> but the memory is the smell & taste,
> when Drunk is just limp, waking
> in beds to retrace steps, still

                              an insoluble phrase.

*

Drunk is frustrated by zeroes & ones,
he wants to equate imperfection;

      handshakes over high fives,
      awkward passing a glance
      in the sterile hallway, paranoia
      checking the reflections of store-
      -front windows & what gets skewed
      in the clear-coats of parked cars,
      the way symbol moves a mob
      over a line or thru the traffic light,
      & sign can stand outside in rain
      or shine, in light or an ambient
      glow in the night, Drunk is afraid
      of next & stays up some nights
      trying to decipher the echoes

                        in the dark.

*

Drunk is never finished with tragedy,
he jumps from character to object;

>   the shot is still a pop-bang, whether
>   tonic chased with vodka, what could be
>   a backfire or Plato & philosopher-kings
>   coming with modern equipment, while
>   out on the back porch nothing can be said
>   below the crowd of crows in the disco
>   of the elm & the shade. The guns are held
>   by the trembling flesh, the places
>   Drunk can't go.

#3

Drunk is excused from jury duty
for the present court term;

        wherever in the woods the I
        presents itself, thought needs
        an action—nomadic signals—kill,
        carry, discuss home—sustain—
        but Sign bucked at Symbol
        over syllables in the marrow,
        so Drunk, still wild then, came
        between the gristle of the ash
        fallen on new matters. Arranging

                            a child & stick.

*

Drunk returns to work tomorrow to write
quantum equations & associative gibberish;

      the leaves bud as atoms bang, push,
      & knock out of these bonds, nothing
      is but the opposite of what couldn't
      take, so Drunk waits on lies
                             to recede.

*

Drunk is in-particular tonight & functions
for the poet or the pagan;

>   the dried red, peeling yellow, on blue
>   & green dust—the day of Father Illogix
>   in the motions of a master class, flame
>   is released on a rally of hydrogen,
>   figures of pok-a-dot, a way toward "-ou"
>   & how do, what I am called, Drunk
>   has trouble bending the tongue, over
>   crossed brow, he—year five—tells Illogix
>   "Je suis le chiffre huit tombé sur mon coté"
>   & smiles, "Quel age as-tu?" Illogix is a lone ember
>   of mid afternoon.

*

Drunk defines a strategy like weasels,
lovers & enemies of an intimate grate;

      every Sunday the delegates are a trot
      out on key market blocks with smudged
      ties between sugar coated lapels. No
      one knows what to bid as these laws
      will not ratify the word, advocate. They're
      in a raft; in the woods; becoming familiar
      to the growth of a falling shadow
      above & below. Matters of altitude.
      While the eagle descends upon rodents
      living in a world of ocean, Drunk seizes
      the throat & is taken

                                       upward.

*

Drunk is often in such phrases transporting
what sounds a grunt calls language;

       tonight the river is high on the bank
       clever thoughts hang behind
       some slurred smiles with the adolescent-
       -years-old & two-thirds adult. Drunk
       stands in a red shirt smiling. Woman
       walks by the humidity of bodies,
       takes the glass from Drunk's hands
       as sense vibrates between dance & those
       more primal pitches. All movement,
       & whatever sound, static waves
       revolving out from the glance held

                      by Drunk & Woman.

*

Drunk confines himself to second best,
he infers; the moment is recognized;

   Plato trembled holding creosote,
   no matter what combat he applied
   to the question & thus a failed poet;
   sure, it's holy & the something
   whispers spirit—imagine the arm
   that holds the iron to the flame,
   not the heat nor the pain, the steady
   wanton love of Drunk, staring

           over fire.

*

Drunk is taking a smoke break
& will not return for an hour or more;

      in a step out the door a red tailed
      hawk tears down from
      the limb to take another
      squirrel caught staring into the city
      drain just as Drunk decided this

                    is the exit.

#4

Drunk set about raising a bed of dirt,
& after the food, planted Bee Balm in a row;

      the children brought forks & knives
      the dogs dug up the onions & pissed
      on the tomatoes, but in the hour of dusk
      Drunk saw the hummingbirds hover above
                          the torn leaves.

*

Drunk is cleaning directive fissures
in the reactions of hyperbolic structures;

       son absorbs each impulse gone
       to heat, a bond of martyrs & the belief
       to which gods with leaps of reality
       make in casts named pure; Drunk knows
       these fallen knees ache like artifact
       even in days when structures crumble,
       but remain the fragment
                              emitting neutrons.

*

Drunk is a liar's riot at decibels
formed by a cradle treading water;

   a rake in hand to tend the flames
   as Illogix finds the dead burning
   trash—a daily brush-your-teeth, say-
   your-prayers-kind off thing—& spits
   out gas as he rants about cat food,
   hell, how waste is contained; the last
   thing left will be the melted tin
   containers of industry standards
   for Illogix to burn, Illogix to collect;
   Drunk smiles & the hair on the back
   of his neck says to agree, but then there
   are the forms becoming;
        emblems of absence
          within the coals.

*

Drunk—came to kill & watch the decay,
but there was the wait to endure;

       (find) take future, destroy the last letter
       "e," subtract the "you're," hold it close,
       protect what inflections steal, & wait
       for the hyenas to step all innocent like,
       as one comes forward, the pack hides,
       because they're beasts of conjecture
       & willing to test a patience of stand;
       while they laugh beneath razor smiles,
       Drunk never thought with a carcass
       at his feet to be any such lion, any word,
       just a set of abbreviations for enclitic
       names he refuses to pronounce
                       in his own
                               decayed orbit.

*

Drunk walks inconsistent, an inferior need
to stare, & thus is banished with poets;

> what relics howitzers make, rust
> & sand, just beyond that old sea,
> what monuments house the discarded
> shells, how hollow cannons & torpedo
> tubes whistle spirituals of forgotten,
> philosophers fallen. Drunk writes
> now in blood, never, never, hell,
> to mock, imitate, or recreate

those ravenous kings.

*

Drunk never returned to work after the tree
rat died, just shook, took the keys & drove;

      the needle fell across the gauge, three
      hundred miles today, the light yellow,
      & with an empty wallet, Drunk
      argued about love with a clerk &

                        left on foot.

*

Drunk never perceives anything fully
or comprehends completely;

        absolute temperature is a direct
        proportion to what molecules wander
        the uncounted blocks for tangent problems
        with inscribed angles to a singular point
        where a young man finds himself
        at a door that he wants to be familiar
        even as his hand hesitates to knock;
        the momentum of desire to be
        a provocative prick in the tender
        moments of Woman's room; the fear
        beneath his cowl. What can Drunk bury
        in a week? All his audible murmurs

                        pronounced.

Our Etymology

Some days, I wonder who bore you,
were you a thought lingering
in my head, or was it some
night that I tucked too far away
to remember, when you with that
silly grin all covered in life,
stepped from Woman's womb?

No, I presume there where times
before that; I wasn't
the only son in this world. Is that
why you kept playing
around with a neuter tongue,
laughing *I is it*, when he
kept wanting you to call him Father?

I get it. No beginnings for an indefinite
self. Alright, so *Fuck Him*. He can
keep his romantic vowels; we'll pull
the arrow & pluck the ewe. 'Cause
Seems to me time came when you
made a choice; suppose I can understand
the who; the gods can't even touch

her & she's well aware of you, me,
what she did. But I don't
know if we often remember who
you were before, or me.
See, it's been years now since any
such altercation, I don't swing
at things much anymore, so tell me,
                              how did we

                                        do that Drunk?

#5

Drunk is a bush soul to each abstract;
his counter, the lone dog tracking home;

      take a zero & brush off another;
      take a breath; Drunk is told to stay
      out of the hemming & hawing
      between Sign & Symbol, he orders
      another; whatever the quality, no matter
      the presence, Drunk watches sit,
      drink & depart; elements come with
      their fears, or hesitance, they order
      a drink, nibble an appetizer, & speak
      with winks, laughter, looks here, some
      there, share what they can, & leave
      tucked into one another, Drunk is

                    a long stare.

*

Drunk set about painting a portrait
today with a brush labeled *the dawn*;

> every pedal blade & leaf covered
> with pollen, concrete yellow,
> cars all dull, & the sun was
> supposed to be a golden light rising
> with the shadows of last night
> in their syn-, a few patches con-
> curls of expression while the crows
> kip, squawk, croak, God's little
>
>   joke on Drunk.

*

Drunk keeps colors with borders, & maps
out his own meteoric plummet;

       somewhere before the salad bowl was
       a projectile to take out the dining room
       wall, & Mother Orchid made it
       home; before Illogix tumbled along
       the natural slope of the hill & played
       ping-pong with the trickle of blood
       from his scalp; before Drunk decided
       to nibble carrots & watch the last
       steps, Illogix was a broken son
       trying to fix the heavy hand of his

                           own father.

*

Drunk is effective between phobias & panic
but suffers without attack; poems have skipped

                                            across the street;

          human as is, with head on a pivot,
          conscious spins—spinning—over fire
          & an inner interrogation; the right arm is
          numb, not the left, so the heart is not
          likely to burn out?; why does the pinky
          over there shake & the pointer on the left
          seems unlikely to move? Perhaps it is
          an aneurism; that itch, the one,
          an inch above the ear & three back
          toward the stem, is that the first sign? Drunk
          is losing ideas to the people buying
          clothes—hours later—burnt outside
          where last call is a one minute warning,
          & highballs are two ounces
                                            self medication.

*

Drunk is the thin light bathing the room
translated into a momentum of focus;

       an easier place to fall when it doesn't
       take Woman long to see what phone calls
       are ignored, how Illogix can be
       dismissed, but flags his son's heart
       to circulate the guilt; Woman watches
       the table lamp cast the silhouette
       while Drunk snivels on the edge
                        of the bed.

*

Drunk is never immediate, but still reacts
as he cannot know his own substance;

        someone weaves a basket with twine
        & cedar strips, everyone in the camp takes
        turns carrying the last remarks of poetry;
        just over the next ridge Plato delivers
        a speech on art as magic & how it weakens
        the mind, an inconsistent sight; Drunk draws
        a symbol or poem in the earth to prepare
                            the last stand.

*

Drunk is a swing to point of view, a panic,
to say this, but see the self do that;

> those boys are throwing feces
> at a house, which hours ago
> was a daydream in passing—here
> in the city children ran around
> the sixteen cubic feet between the door
> & the sidewalk, something felt
> special—those boys say that this house
> called the cops on last week's party—
> that is revolt—& this Drunk is
> a long rant for the street to hear;
> he threatens, stomps, raises hands
> to the sky, & as those boys walk
> away, Drunk is ready to be a child,
> a kid, 5 or 21 years of muster, but not
> a lot of thought, so Drunk drops trou
> calling to settle these disputes with
> some more meaningless

measurement.

The Palaver

It's a pink-fairy-armadillo, that's
what I saw when I left the cave, but when
I returned in my way, all I had were some
grunts & crude ochre to throw
on the wall. So Drunk, it's time we take a walk;
whatever you are; whatever I think
I am, Lord knows you got the means

to make a universe, hell,
at least offer us
a reason or two. It's true. I'm liable
to burn a hash mark into the paper,
call it a figure—humph & shit
—might even draw your face;
so what, so how, & so why?

Patience. I'll bet you can
measure that in sips from the Ball jar;
a little line here sure to meet a loop
out there. On a side note, leprosy
might come from certain types of armadillo
meat. Regardless, I'm not here for food;
so often I bend you,

when I'm looking to use;
man sets out upon the earth, & finds himself
a plow. So of course I found time
to enunciate, some symbol or sign—
to run my tongue across the hard palate—
& the audience shook their heads,
but I know what I saw, & you were there
                                        when I tried.

Baring Torn Roots

With a *caw-ah* & all other words forgotten;
on dark wings come Drunk's words of the dawn;

                the murder follows the battered
                woman below, crawling through
                the wood. After a night of romance
                & the hands of her husband, ending
                the way they always do, with him
                chambering his thirty-aught of pride,
                only to shout & pass out in his
                Laz-y-boy. Tonight, she picks herself
                up off the living room floor & makes
                for the Elm, with broken fingers
                she tears a white Orchid from
                the garden & keeps on muttering
                her prayers until she reaches the tree;
                gelds the lower sepals & reaches
                into her womb taking all that she can.
                Then with blood & tattered petals
                she begins to write
                                          in the dirt.

#6

Drunk is prone to drink, a terminal
lobe or padded head on the tendons of I;

> what checked with Sign & decided
> to order one more pattern for pouring
> raw thoughts over a hunger that will
> not be limited, what read Symbol
> gesturing at the bushy tails & short
> skirts of passing particles, with pictures
> to explain the method of want—how
> wishes come with higher proof & a slow
> clap to finish the statement; Drunk sips
> for when debts are written as names
> ~~that take me.~~

*

Drunk proposed a love affair with a cloud,
God took some seven days to decide;

> sins are the flesh to bare the ought
> or will be soon; vines so often try
> to survive—a stem crawls with leaves
> that skim unknown imperfections,
> whose bark the tree identifies as self,
> & with hair the vines bite into the tender
> pulp; Drunk, like Apollo, is clamoring
> to a love who will remain rooted; God
> is frantic & pacing between Alpha,
> Omega, & Earth, with an ear for
> prayer, trying to decide the winners
> of Sunday's ball games & wars; Drunk
> sucks the venom out of the remnants
>   & open wounds.

*

Drunk stood with a glass of laughter,
thought himself a crowd; the armless beast;

      the light across the deck glanced
      a morning the way land can look up
      in the quiet hours, say something
      fragile;

            faith;

      Drunk is thinking Illogix. This is
      a moment for the Appalachian born
      boy. Twilight is peaceful until
      the mountain lion speaks a valley,
      some series of peaks in a distance
      shutter. That terrifying man. Drunk
      knows the story; a boy hops the fence
      before his last game; sitting alone
      in the stands, playing out every
      possible; a beast prepared for tidily-
      -winks. But in a lifetime of night
      terrors he would pencil in *son* when
      asked to describe his fears. Another
      boy whose seen him fall from a tree
      with a chainsaw & sit down to dinner.
      To do the most of mother's table—
      in a junkyard now—leaving a plate
      on its edge. All the while *you* is a word
      like *me*, Drunk mumbles in a mouthful
      of carrots,

                           unable to say.

*

Drunk means & doesn't mean, Drunk is
a means. Most days Drunk is mean

      to his letter siblings; cases
                                 lower & upper
              alike;
     Drunk thinks himself some kind of
     dark knight, the dusted rider with six
     syllables on his hip;
                               smoke & fire,
     the cloud in his suffix; the dirt,
     the note, the stem, or the chaw
                             stuck in his lip;
     all the while Drunk is frantic
     to human touch as a means
                                    for breath to fall.

*

Drunk will not project, betray, or dangle
patient smiles; no, Drunk will go down there
                                    & lick
                                        love;

                    a   t o u c h;
            petal   holds onto   hope
        the way   a child walks   with bare feet
    for the   stroke   of each   blade; to be just
    the act;   what we grow to forget—the heart
open & imperfect   unfasten, undone, naked
    Drunk   be-   -comes following Woman
        down the path, her hands   trace along
            the wall till she reaches the handle,
            smiles;   release   takes;
                passion as the seed
                    comes alive
                    with what
                        we
                    took
                        &
                    called
                    love;
                    what
                    rot
            we   left   by
        the hand   with   what-
            ever   could   be
            just   above   the
            thought; &   take
                    now
            like some god rose, or arose, what is,
            can be hail or rain coming for a me,
                while Woman & Drunk hold onto
                the dirt they find in their hands
                making holes, hope for seeds
            within this burial, which is to say,
            the white blank page or ritual;
            the masks I wear to open the door,

71

no,
I am able;

in passion they pray.

Drunk will get you home no matter what
is draped across these syllabic cranes;

     eh!, said the distinct self to the selbaz,
     so what if we diverted the water thief

                      o
                     n
                       e,
                    o-
                   -r
                    t
                    w
                    o

           c
            o
           n
            c
           e
           r
           n
          s
          before   the   whistle
       blew?   ten more   or so
          minutes   per day
for an hour overtime; the $ that looks like
an empty wallet or point where the weight
of the soul is measured by this one blood
vile, this Petri dish of excrement, a blotter
full of Drunk's chromatic half shell in color

Drunk,
          compartment of subterfuge,

counts the breaths; a stem crawls from the earth,
finds time to make a petal or a few; wait on the light,
pray for hope or rain; Drunk keeps
                 counting.

Pouring His Own Glass

Drunk will wag & shh, yet find
the not so often sigil leashed

by war, the this & that. He looks
at scars, taking measure, judging

their nothing & Drunk keeps
wanting a beard, but I say no;

he don't know how to stroke
or wakeup screaming Delilah.

Sure he attempts a coherent
picture for it be nothing more

than hair to him; something else
to shave away. Drunk has curls

of red hair & his kin say he's lucky.
But then he wants some recent—

something growing, boy says Ike
again & again—notion. Still, that

scar across his eye & scab of nose
make Drunk beautiful to livers'

& breathers'; he keep thinking
himself special, trying to hide

history behind hair. Drunk's all
vain in the evening; accumulation

handed down.

#7

Drunk is the wave function, a probable
account for maximum potential;

$$\Psi(\mathbf{x}, t) = A e^{i(\mathbf{k}\cdot\mathbf{x}-\omega t)}$$
where speech is a variable
before time; the latent anxieties
took all the mutter with stern
hammer, groans in like grumbles;

since $\dfrac{\partial}{\partial t}\Psi = -i\omega\Psi$ realize

then that the lavender is kinetic
taking over the corner in a city plot
with speech determinates; potential
weeds braiding roots;

$i\hbar\dfrac{\partial}{\partial t}\Psi = -\dfrac{\hbar^2}{2m}\nabla^2\Psi + V\Psi$ so that
we are velocity or repetition
at a glance lost by he who goes
there & she who is coming this
on a sidewalk as particle is being,
taking this plane, where on
another, they lock arms now,
turn heads; presence, the two spin,
along some momentum;

Drunk now.

*

Drunk survives the birth rites of dirt;
he acts out observances of the flesh;

> In a father's eyes lowering the machine
> against a half fallen tree; seven crows
> took off, squawks north; Drunk would
> remember this as the boy who only stepped
> closer to the shutter of Illogix & the engine,
> pulp & chips, the fabricated extension
> of humanity biting, chewing, tearing
> at the earthen project; eight or nine, Drunk
> still recalls how patient the sunlight of that
> midmorning seemed; the tiny feet
> down hill; the weight in the canopy—
> final—the crack, mid seconds of the fall,
> the boughs that took the boy; darkness;
>   the image I want
>   to remember as Father.

*

While Drunk can't say David, nor place
a charge in the sling & shake a world

> by some pathetic little wound; Drunk
> built a fire—an ember or figure
> waiting for the sky to meet
> the plume; the jet-fuel remnant
> from a plane I never saw,
> which is to say, Drunk didn't
> need a myth. Woman sat down
> to lie against a stalk & Drunk was

read aloud.

*

for Mr. Beckett

　　　Drunk. *Say* Drunk. *Be said* Drunk. *Somehow* Drunk.
Till nohow Drunk. *Said nohow* Drunk.

　　　Star is thief tonight with the crumb trails of dark
matter. Equations call or pray for the late-shift prostitute
who wags her finger to the soft accents in the numerals
& weaker particles falling behind the bathroom door
with pant legs at the ankles or angles, as a variable, which
is to say the hand, is holding a discharged member;
the illuminous light.

　　　NO SAYS the SIGN. NO VACANCIES for him & his
portraiture—the order of signals is a predator seeking
a means for Drunk to make landfall, or crash-down, dust
to rise, a good bit of flame, ash & creosote, some way to
preserve the flesh for this assembly, the blind spectators
who pause for a sound, for a mark to touch, for simply Drunk.

　　　Blanks for when Drunk*'s gone. When nohow* Drunk.
Drunk *all seen as only* Drunk. *Undimmed.*

*

At the gate, Drunk looks out, judging the path
with a small town ticket, speaking my name—

every sur-, nom-, & cog—all that I
can declare—in his hands are reins that will

lead a dirt stained mare down a trail I don't
know if I can step upon with my head

leaning forward anymore. I set a camp
& tend the fire while my wife, the one Drunk

calls Woman, needs me to find a spider
& kill or tear off those appendages

that chew. Drunk never dismounts, but I am
not alone now. I keep digging foundations,

while my Drunk's eyes are never able
to leave the roots or language of a road

                                        ahead.

Epilogue

Drunk looks out for night to nod toward
day, as inferior as a rally is to raise a ?

      by dawn, the carbon copies approach
      noble thoughts & palaver with being;
                      what shrapnel is
                      unleashed past
                      arrowheads, miss-
                      -thrown spears,
                      blood lines of steel;
                      hear the pow, lofty
                      crack, the heart;
                      macho Americano,
                      kill-slaughter-slay-
  war is stone,   -butcher; do your best
                      to pay the toll.
  it endures,

      the great utensil arrives,
      while Drunk must be a Drunk,
      & allow me to be on the plane
      as unwitting flesh, a simple man…
                  I leave
                  Drunk
                  behind;
        this western resonance—how ever late—
      of kings; the philosopher & his dirt, no matter
        the water he wields; here is Plato's head
              on a pike,
             but we don't
             need to see
           a star explode;
       we forget we are poets & smile as this
    all comes to an end; I look back at Drunk, his
    eyes on the process of now, where war is not
    a rational for me, what ever head or thought
     is raised; I am dumb, Drunk's eyes close.

Notes

Drunk | wərd |

n.-a single divergent thought or element in speech
& text, used with others (but often alone) to form
a sentence & typically written or printed;
eternity on either side.

• a one off, distinct, conceptual unit of language,
comprising of inflected & variant forms; what
the tongue betrays.

| ˌsēmēˈätiks, ˌsemē-, ˌsemˌī- | pl. n [treated as sing.]
• the study of signs & symbols, how they play in the dark.

| əˈskēsis | (also ascesis | əˈsēsis | n.
• the practice of severe self-discipline, typically for personal
reasons. Often causes one to submit a leave of absence
to daylight, or the latent hours.

| ˈpōətrē, ˈpōitrē | n.
• a special intensity given to the expression & ideas
by the use of a distinctive style & this walk;
a sometimes strut.

• The quality of heart rate & what passion a pen can
withstand to be regarded as the well-built-pipe forming
the only hypothetical feature between all, I, now & the
space of you, a compact region of earth, stardust,
& nothing; boundaries from I to you & all
parts of the body; whisper the way, what will of this
word, me, bridge, where I say love—we read the Drunk—
                    the earth listens,
                            says,

                                    ok, alright,
                                    be cool, take
                                    a long day,

enjoy the night;what
Drunk will

find.

The implement
or tool.

Just a Drunk.

ABOUT THE AUTHOR

Ian Bodkin received his MFA in Poetry from Vermont College of Fine Arts. His work has appeared in *Marco Polo Arts Magazine*, *Atlas & Alice*, *Rain Taxi*, and *scissors and spackle* among others. He teaches writing and literature at both a high school and community college in Richmond, VA.